Do You Remember Love & Poetry?

More Love Poems
by Karl Stuber

To Chelsea.

Thanks to Kristin Ell for help with back cover text.

Do you remember Love and Poetry?

Poetry exists without love often
It started as a good way to spread news
The harsh reality it would soften
Plus stop listeners from taking a snooze

Would be easier for one to recall
Whether it was the author who wrote it
Or being passed <maybe> on to Nepal
Love can exist without poetry lit

Not a poem needs to pass between pairs
For love itself is poetry when real
In touches, loving sighs and the soft stares
Lovers learn to know how a heart should feel

With love and poems we'll have it both ways
We'll share our true feeling throughout our days

Milady

Your goofy smile did me a world of good
One day your smile changed to the tight lipped kind
Showed my smile was not doing all It could
I had to figure what was on your mind

Couldn't think of a thing, though I racked my brain
I didn't miss there was something I should do
Utter a superlative, I abstain
If did nothing, I'd still be liked by you

My respect for you is from recalling
That in past troubles you showed "I got this"
Answer to your problem is soon calling
Knowing you'd work it out hit like a kiss

That's how I'd want to feel to the lady
Near me, so I smiled at milady

❦

Promise eyes

I do try to keep all my promises
At least the ones I realized I made
Promise made with eyes break like rock schistous
With something simple like sunglasses shade

Told you of my plans of a time and place
That I'd be at when it seemed you'd be there
Or going to an event you'd embrace
Wouldn't dare to think of us there as a pair

But looking back I can certainly see
With my promise eyes it could be mistook
As a forward to being forwardly
Based on you perception of my outlook

Thinking there's promise in my eyes is true
Hope future holds promises kept to you

Sense of love

Can't be easy to believe love is true
Love's amazing! What are the odds against
Us being ready to love here unto
Was it that you'd be tender that I sensed

I did sense kindness and understanding
Was all part of the way you looked and spoke
Saw a smile days when life was demanding
Knew that you'd always be a gentle folk

I have not missed you have a sense of will
You use to make the world a better place
Can tell your sense of fun is versatile
Holding back feelings, that you don't embrace

I admire that you have a lot of sense
And still you enjoy the fun of nonsense

Beautiful grows

I'm sure slow to tell you "you're beautiful"
Even though it's true, we've a ways to go
Those times we have talks that are meaningful
I see you become more lovely aglow

When I say you are beautiful it's new
An improved version of your loveliness
"Getting good, soft and bright" reads the review
The well of your beauty is bottomless

When I tell you you're beautiful I'll add
Another adjective to mind's record
I'll take a chance so as to make you glad
Head full of adjectives is my reward

You'll be a brilliantly heart-glad firebrand
Gracefully sparkling clear from wonderland

Growing memory

Did you get any bruises when you hit
The ground, I heard no whump saw no feather
As sound mute your softness would benefit
Without your wings peering at the heather

You leaned too far and fell off of your cloud
To me it seems you came out of nowhere
Suddenly you're walking beside me proud
All others think you were already there

Living like everyone else on earth
With history and a life here all made
Your magic is giving me a rebirth
My memories becoming overlaid

It's getting to the point where I'll construe
That I have not had a life without you

Fear of affection

Why am I horrified by attention
I am afraid of thoughts of affection
When thinking of you, hope for defection
To choose you would be a fine selection

I certainly can not claim frustration
That comes from failed effort not inaction
All I've shown was lack of motivation
No sense, you're full of beautification

My fault, my hopes in a constellation
Were put by me, that formed a causation
Made me want my hopes in a cessation
Care about you should be my vocation

Just too scared of possible deflation
Some day I'll show someone adoration

No tether

I was being nice, not being needy
When thanking you for our time together
Expecting any more would be greedy
Know you got to go, I hold no tether

Telling you how you being next to me
Helps lighten my load, was not intended
To shame you to stay, want you to feel free
When you go, I will not be offended

In life often failed to show gratitude
I was too busy enjoying the joy
From the kindness better than solitude
Want to thank without appearing to cloy

I hope you go on about your business
I'm flush with afterglow of your nearness

Expect pain

Afraid to try to love someone for fear
Of someone's heart getting broke in pieces
I do keep noticing lonely folks here
Do they fret of effects if love ceases

Fear is there to save me from hurt that's real
But the fear of hurt affects me so much
Like a cringe from a far off thunder peel
No reason, I've never felt lightning's touch

Those times I suffer a pain it seems less
Than the imaginary hurt I felt
Thinking about future pain, what a mess
How do I get over the hand I'm dealt

I have made bad picks. After love was spurned
Fear made me miss true heart I could have learned

2ⁿᵈ chance valentines

Miss chance to dance, there will be other dances
Always do-overs, other side of night
Imagine life without second-chances
And not even a do-over in sight

Anniversary, Birthday, Valentine's
One chance a year to show your love on those
Or one chance to not cut heart's binding twines
If you forget gift and even a rose

Second chance Valentine's Day the world needs
Especially if it's a Saturday
March fourteenth ideal for valentines deeds
Leap year we can use Sadie Hawkins day

Memories of valentine's day still fresh
Creating second chance for hearts to mesh

True love awaits

Hope I don't cause a misunderstanding
By thinking you have a heart that is strong
And don't feel the need to be partnering
Only so that you can feel you belong

I've been treating you like someone who waits
For someone you understand and in kind
They'd be one who discerns you and your traits
The way it is with me, I'd feel a bind

To be with one to stop being alone
Then meet one who is a mate of my soul
If I broke a heart feel need to atone
Hate to leave one with a heart less then whole

You feel the same you could be my soul mate
Stand by, for true love they'll be a short wait

Dialogue

Sorry! Stomped your foot, looking for my bus.
Yeah my bus to campus is always late.
Well mine's on time when I'm late, makes me cuss.
"Tee Hee" I'm like that. Then you have to wait.

Wait would be nice right now, Alan's my name.
I'm Alana! Next at the name depot.
Weird meeting one who's name's almost the same.
Yeah unless you meet a lot of people.

I bet a lot of guys try to meet you.
Yeah they step on my foot at a bus stop.
Oh! Alana that I didn't mean to do.
Kidding! Wait! We're victims of an eavesdrop.

How long have they been listening, zounds!
While we spoke a hundred and forty sounds.

෴

A bit hurt

It may seem a bit strange that I have not
Tried with all my might to date you sooner
Obviously your attention I got
Didn't cringe at my attempt as a crooner

I've wondered why you're attracted to me
Not a problem, I think it is your heart
That has drawn you to me and can't get free
You showed faith and trust in me at the start

I really just thought I was a close friend
Certainly not any chance of romance
The caring you showed I didn't comprehend
Til' between us there became a distance

Lacked experience, didn't know what to do
Us being close seemed too good to be true

Strength

The strength I receive from thinking of you
Assists me in many ways big and small
Limits the frustration from things I do
When stymied your name I silently call

When opening a jar for the first time
I usually rap it on the counter
But once after others had their bedtime
That task there was a quiet encounter

I tried with all my might to open it
But I could just not budge it in the night
Said your name softly and it did submit
In my head the thought I had was alright!

Past times said your name to make a light load
That is something I value more than gold

Sag (of our sofa)

When I sit I am in a lonely sag
That is when I wish you were sitting here
Our hips together lounging at day's lag
Talk of thoughts and feelings, our hearts are near

As we speak of the things we've discovered
That grow in our hearts when love waters them
The pleasant memories we've recovered
Our new feelings replace love's requiem

We two enjoying a lively discourse
About our new way of looking at life
So as to uncover what's at it's source
Could be no more than an absence of strife

Sharing a sag is what love means to me
The best way to be together glue free

Sleeping elephants

Relationship that I want to increase
Question of making love would be silent
Like a hued elephant sleeping in peace
To leave it that way we're each well-content

We'd both be happy with intimacy
Experienced by talks full of feeling
And old thoughts arising from dormancy
Punctuated by kisses, self-healing

Our past heartbreaks, and slight touches showing
That hearts are matching with every word
Wait until our love is overflowing
Like a waterfall with a humming bird

Flitting around the honeysuckle blooms
Hearts open as elephant turns to fumes

Infatuation

If Infatuation is felt by one
By some it might be described as a crush
Like it is puppy love and just for fun
Feelings can't be swept away with a brush

Infatuation shared is like a crash
They both are totaled, hearts bent out of shape
Heart's no longer their own, part of a mash
Love holds their hearts together with no tape

Each others heart becomes an attachment
Hearts together in a pair sharing all
That feelings hold, no need for detachment
Living their shared lives eyeball to eyeball

Dealing with strong feelings can't be easy
That is unless they're shared, then it's breezy

Calm days await(Add me to you)

You may feel you think too much about me
I may feel I think too much about you
But too plus too equals for, could it be
You're just right for me I'm just right for you

I think we add up, it's one plus three, though
Think my one and your one add up to for
Counting us as a pair, for love will grow
That can't be measured by an auditor

To count our love's amount no one could teach
But I know to me you certainly count
Til I met you, felt love was out of reach
Want love that's sincere, Your love I won't flaunt

Your love is much better than any pun
I anxiously await days halcyon

Love kind

People often talk about making love
I talk like our love is made in our hearts
No need to make love to fit like a glove
But someday our love may be off the charts

That sure would be something to celebrate
I am holding out for that day, til' then
I will continue to be cerebrate
About I'm needing you like oxygen

My feelings for you go way beyond lust
Though to deny lust is to deny life
Feelings of respect cover it like dust
Feelings remain, not cut out with a knife

Think we'll fit together when we nuzzle
Like matched pieces from a jigsaw puzzle

VIP

I only feel important in your eyes
Even though others may look me straight on
In those eyes I can not discern from lies
Things they attest to were said in boredom

Delivered with made up sincerity
But with you truth shows when I look your way
I think it may be called integrity
You are not striving to impress each day

Just striving to complete taken on task
To satisfy yourself you did your best
Won't quit until you're done. None have to ask
Strength of your willpower is put to test

Still you have time for questions asked by me
Giving well thought opinions not shyly

Not Yet Dear

"Not Yet" is a phrase rumored to cause some
Friction in a marriage, after question
Did you take out the trash, fix the vacuum
Mow the lawn, check lights, clear sink's congestion

Which could someday cause the marriage to end
But would the marriage exist without it
Said "Not Yet" when asked have you a boyfriend
Some things that first charm turn to opposite

But if you are in sales and on a call
When you're asking "have you tried our products"
You hear "not yet" could be future windfall
In business it's not something that obstructs

Like all words, they have no assigned value
It's feelings behind them that give them hue

Near night

Setting sun shines shimmering silver sage
After an atmospheric act arose
Beginning beaming bright, best be backstage
Perfecting perpendicular pair pose

Day doze draws deeply dramatically
Evening's excitation's euphoria
Loving life's last limitless loyalty
Imagination's infusoria

Familiar freedom's feelings fathom
Calling clear cut characteristic charm
Over obvious obstructions oath Om
Hiding heartfelt hopelessness helps halt harm

Midnight maneuver's motivate morale
Zeals zoological zodiacally

∽

Heart's secrets

My mind does not know my heart, fantastic
I'm sure that's a cliche, I can't recall
It seems new and exciting, bombastic
It's like a science fiction free-for-all

Violating all the rules of physics
Was a glimpse through a door to a new world
You could open without aid of mystics
I thought I knew my heart but it unfurled

I told you things I had not thought to say
Had you guessed my heart felt that way, did my
Heart sense your heart was open by a ray
Emulating out to me, won't ask why

The key to that door in your hands and heart
Hold mine to explore, that will be a start

That

I told you once I wouldn't be as happy
If you were not around and it is true
I hope with all my heart<heart that's sappy>
That you are doing what is best for you

That thought makes me proud and it gives me strength
I'd feel weak if I thought for a minute
That you're pining for me all the day's length
I'd quit poems, learn to play the spinet

Just thought you were too great for me to hold
You listened to me and became my champ
Personality I saw was not cold
I feared my feelings seemed those of a scamp

So I acted like I was made of ice
Saw signs that said you were just being nice

Love 101

I can say this knowing no girl will take
It as a challenge to become Mrs.
I'm looking for a summer love no fake
That would not get past tentative kisses

Soft touches caused by us two feeling kind
Sitting close together as she speaks cool
About her heart, our fingers entwined,
Tiny kisses; dancing close like High School

She'd feel my excitement and not comment
She would know I will still be around her
If she pretended there's no excitement
Our feelings of romance we will defer

That's how folks learned about love as they grew
Like to learn about love that way with you

Tee Shirt

Since we have met, about you all I know
Of things you have done is from your tee shirts
I want to know the real you who will show
Without questions guys would ask to be flirts

Heard those, what's your major, what job you want
Where you hope to live, do you have brothers
Or sisters, what restaurants do you haunt
What's your zodiac sign, among others

It is not the things you do and have done
It is the person you are beneath that
With heart for caring and fondness for fun
Shows we would always make a concordat

I didn't need to ask to find those things out
Just treated you with respect when about

Years pass

People ask what we could have in common
With our ages being so far apart
We both feel in love you should have some fun
We do care deeply for each others heart

We share a like appetite for all things
We have found in the world surrounding us
Excited to see what the next day brings
Facing each one with hearts magnanimous

We're lucky the only differences
Between us may be generational
Some of like age have interferences
That to us sometimes seem irrational

Neither of our lives controlled by our peers
Something that won't change with the passing years

Rock solid

Did I promise the top of a mountain
Guess I did because that's where I'm going
Did I promise a youth saving fountain
I guess I did, something has me glowing

Did I promise Christmas every day
Guess I did anticipation will grow
Did I promise next day the joy would stay
I guess I did no letdown will we know

Did I promise each day you'll laugh so much
Guess I did there is a smile on your face
Did I promise you stars the moon and such
I guess I did they're above us in space

Did I promise to be here ever more
I Guess I did here I am like I swore

Gentle

I am too gentle for this world we're in
My stuttering I have not yet conquered
Search my heart when I speak below the din
Won't be pushy unless to save or get

Someone from harm when there is no one else
Brave enough to put themselves on knife line
Removing life's pain with heart made scalpels
Treasure times I could be someone's lifeline

You know when you see someone in the street
Who has trouble their two hands can't handle
They will not refuse any help they meet
May got caught by the joke of a vandal

They say without me it would have been rough
Guess too gentle is just gentle enough

Seams sad

My eyes see beauty but my heart feels sad
Sad is a place-keeper for future love
Keep the heart clear, later love can en-glad
Envy, jealousy, schadenfreude, self-love

To prefer those over sad is tempting
Sad can stop them from getting a foothold
To explain, this poem is attempting
Sad has no envy, nothing others hold

Could bring joy, jealousy does not exist
With nothing to lose, can't lose a fortune
Sad and schadenfreude can not co-exist
Sad sees kinship in others misfortune

It's hard to love someone sad, it does seem
Self-love's out, Real love can get through the seam

Linear living

Don't seem to be into linear living
Past, present and future all together
Each reaction hedged by not forgiving
Myself for failed words and actions, whether

They were improper words or inactions
Encouraged by memories of the past
And acts tempered by current distractions
With worries of having effects that last

Those really are all good things if done right
Learn from past mistakes to see how it's done
We know it's a warning when we feel fright
Should we back off or proceed with caution

Recalling all like actions helps you judge
I hold memories like some hold a grudge

Genuine

My foot in mouth disease is what's at fault
For us not getting off on the right foot
I seemed a loser, you too by default
Seemed best to ignore you, not pussy foot

But then I saw you face the rain with style
Without meaning to I gave you a grin
You gave me an "I'm all wet, so what" smile
My heart felt "There's a girl who's genuine

She's just like me, she does not like to shirk
Feelings of negativity, she'd squash"
Then one day I looked down the road, at work
And saw a distance figure with panache

As she got close saw it was you hiking
Of all ladies seen you're the most striking

Beautifully deep

I just want to say Hi and see your smile
You've a face that I don't want to ignore
You're afraid what's on my mind all the while
Past guys looking at you were just a bore

They have tried weeks to love you for minutes
From all that you have learned you have insights
For which poets trade their souls, no regrets
I'll keep my soul, you keep your heart and nights

I would just like to hear you think aloud
About those insights and feelings you've learned
Teach me to pick love from "face in the crowd"
Hope you'll learn to give and get love returned

So to find one to love for months and years
I know you deserve that instead of tears

Shy guy

There's that shy guy watching all of the girls
Wishing he could spend time with any one
He can see her all decked out wearing pearls
Laughing with joy at his humor homespun

Girls see him too, standing in the corner
Looking like he got lost from Miss Bo Peep
He is kind of cute would he adorn her
Or not get close cause she'd think he's a creep

To the assertive guy she's just a night
With a girl he had not been with as yet
To the shy guy she is a shining light
And entire life he thought he'd never get

He won't show while she's picked up and let down
And then all she'll have for him is a frown

Island time

Island time is different so I am told
Deadlines are not etched in stone, more like sand
Or with arranged rocks on beach with stones cold
But the clock for love has a New York hand

Very few people will procrastinate
They'd be run over as if by a dray
By those who hurry to get passionate
On islands the only game is love play

Okay folks the preseason is over
Time to get down to a summer of love
Like kids say "come on over red rover"
Get your piece of romance with stars above

There's five weeks of happily forever
Then reality sets in however

Happily forever

A romantic relationship should be
Happily forever no matter how
Long it lasts, it's the best way to love free
It's taking a risk to go all in now

But that should be minimized with some work
At first hold your heart back, learn all you can
If all seems right, with romance go berserk
If doubts appear before love has began

There's nothing lost except breath of a sigh
Also works in "happily forever"
That loses it's happy, just say goodbye
Holding onto the past is not clever

Even those with no fear shirk the unknown
Still better then a love you have outgrown

Nature turns

Is nature turning on each move and mood
There are all those days I keep smiling wide
Clouds go, next stick with a bad attitude
And the storms start moving in like a tide

I seem so sensitive with my mood change
Like I am a living barometer
It's as if my moods I did prearrange
Using a super-sensitometer

Nature does know when I leave off rain gear
Because the sky looked like all storms had cleared
Can not nature watch other people here
But it seems it's not as bad as I feared

I'm in Love and nature watches me move
Nature turns around people in a groove

Zig-Zag

Women's bodies zig wherever men's zag
But also conversely zag where men zig
But times when our minds zig-zag are a drag
Man's stubbornness can make him seem a pig

It's tough when one wants to speak serious
And the other is in a mood to kid
Does not help when you are being spurious
Then say I was teasing, that was not hid

That's "mockery of communication"
Not to mention it is muddling the line
Of a true exchange of information
Sometimes men and women's thoughts don't align

When either one tries to enforce their will
Thinking that they know best, love that can kill

Romantic with hopes

When I've been called a hopeless romantic
Thought it meant getting romance was hopeless
That waiting for true love's an antic
Give up, settle for a tender caress

But I've been having second thoughts on that
Cause it could mean never give up on hope
I'll always be a romantic, caveat
Hopeless is trying to change me I scope

I am stuck with believing in romance
No matter how many times I'm let down
There's a reason for a poor choice perchance
To true love failure is just a countdown

Love and I are on a collision course
I have been living backwards to the source

Tom girl

Rather love a girly-girl or Tomboy
Mine wouldn't be high-maintenance or squeamish
She would dream of romance bringing her joy
That picture of romance she grew up with

On the outside she's all rough and tumble
But inside her heart she's a girly-girl
If she needs, she'd be ready to rumble
And still she gives fanciful thoughts a twirl

I think her ability to be rough
Protects her heart from everlasting hurt
Inside she'd remain tender and not tough
When true love comes her heart would be alert

She'd embrace it with all her Tomboy's length
Hold it in her heart with girly-girl strength

~

Cute button down

Cute as a button, you're under the flaps
Of my heart, can you please fasten it down
Become an attachment to close the gaps
Like tooth's cavity my heart needs a crown

Cover the hollow space, then fill with love
Check carefully often for a sure fit
Find any leaks, tenderness you can shove
In the space, keep your love from leaving it

I sense your heart's fibers are a strong thread
Of character from the warm smile you show
As you tell tale of being embarrassed
I sense no guile and of morals you know

We'd be in a comfort zone with limits
To pace our love and gain some benefits

Sonors

Few girls he sees would fit his lover's play
When one appears he'll pause, silent he'll call
"Be still my heart, you're driving girls away
Your loud beating is disturbing them all"

But to her he will make this testament
When she's around his heart will be swelling
Looks at her having broad and deep extent
Of beauty and visually compelling

That he'd notice her she's been waiting tressed
She's had a poem he wrote long ago
She had been keeping it in her hope chest
Now it's by her chest with hope all aglow

That these two should meet must be in the stars
Did they find each other using sonars

Clock of love

Clock of love has two gears in conjunction
With teeth made out of personalities
Incompatibility stops function
Like when clock's gear's teeth misalign, pities

Go out to the sinking relationship
One and only chance is doomed to backfire
If one takes the tooth and proceeds to rip
Best take care, you might take with it desire

Try and look for compatibility
Before getting too deep over your head
When deep I lose all rationality
Think mish-mash will increase passion instead

And then forget lessons learned from past years
Too late when ears ring with grind of love's gears

Feel free to smile

Could be some are absorbed by the shadows
Those that have lost their smile due to unuse
Lack of smile will drag down looks as face grows
Folks will back off, let them be a recluse

Get a study done on babies growing
Check the symmetry of face when baby
Then keep checking at intervals showing
Any difference between the youths, maybe

It will be found smiling evens a face
Having a frown just makes it become odd
Don't forget circumstances in test case
May be found folks with frowns have hearts untrod

Folks with a smile considered beautiful
May have hurts covered by smile dutiful

Caveman days

You know when a man says he'll do something
Which he never does, It's from caveman times
If a hunter was heard while discussing
Stalking grounds, he might think best to change climes

To prevent over hunting or worse yet
Losing your kill after doing the work
Caveman who lived to spawn learned to abet
Deception, all through time <seen in Artwork>

Great men and women fall to trusted friends
Natural selection occurs by stage
Ancestors learned to never let on ends
While earth continued to increase in age

Use this to purge thoughts cluttering your brain
Say them out loud, those thoughts you won't retain

Burnished sky

Your arrival was with the burnished sky
The golden hues heralded your coming
The clouds showing pink edges furnished by
Clearing of the skies, sun's glow forthcoming

Bits and pieces of showers blown about
Making sure that all is clean before you
Sweet scent of flowers in the air, no doubt
To imagine flower petals in view

To coat the path beneath your tender feet
The gentle wind blows a warming caress
Lovingly felt all over your face sweet
Spring peepers sending up a charmed chorus

Supporting the quiescent trill of songbirds
Through all that your beauty is undeterred

Deft touch

You do have a gentle hand on the switch
It's not punitive that wouldn't be your style
Just an attention getter with a twitch
And it is always done showing a smile

Have you a deft touch with more then one thing
If there's someone you care for deeply
Would you then enjoy the understanding
Not giving in until it's reached cheaply

As opposed to all costs, for instance
Trying too hard to understand could lead
To one thinking you don't trust their brilliance
I digress, back to the point, to succeed

In life do you have the touch that it takes
To prevent being dragged down by heartaches

Glorious sunsets

Ingredients of glorious sunset
Check the sky to taste and go watch, red first
Makes all the prevalent colors sharp set
Yellow and the orange intermixed with a burst

Of the red in trails all over the sky
For extra special spontaneous time
Look for a pink sky sure to beautify
And sure not as rare as it is sublime

If you can get purple to come out soon
I hope you trust the person you are near
Because if you have a free heart, aswoon
You'll be, set to sink into arms sincere

Sunsets are an ever changing present
Opens before you in encompassment

Roses are red

You're a recorder of dazzling sunsets
Their glory must stick to your heart, ROSES
Could not inspire more grace in you, ARE bets
I'd make until I'm in the RED, closes

Your heart to plain, you see VIOLET hues
When no splendor IS about, in your heart
Is rose BLUE blood flowing through that imbues
Your entire body with glamor apart

From that which shows on your face, soaks your feet
With radiance and each step leaves grand prints
The elegance is left in your lungs, sweet.
Exquisite is the air you exhale, hints

At the magnificence found within you
Thought of next day's blue sky while stars astrew

Thoughts and feelings

I hope I get a chance to prove you this
If you were my girl you would be impressed
I just know I'd care bout' more than a kiss
And hoping it leads to being undressed

I would care about your thoughts and feelings
I'd want to hear your dreams both from sleeping
And from living, I picture you squealing
"Karl, guess what I want to do? " And leaping

Into my arms, I'll hear something brilliant
That we would figure out how to achieve
I'd see that you have become resilient
You'd grow as a person, wouldn't think you'd leave

Cause you are too good for me, what I'll think
You're pretty, smart, sweet, self-assured, we link

∽

Older

I was worried cause I'm so much older
Now I know it took some time to build you
Had to get your bone structure right, molder
Had to be found to attach your sinew

And lay out your muscles just right before
Your skin could be made by silkworms working.
Earth's mines searched for jeweled eyes I adore
Picked proper personality perking

Think of all the prototypes that they've had
<Must of taken thirty years to get right>
Then had to find the perfect mom and dad
To meet and make the right child in the night

So you would be in the right place and time
Here we are, let's release the love enzyme

Romance without love

Romance without love just leaves me lonely
I'm just looking for a friend, not romance
If the friendship turns to love, then only
With her heart with me we'll do the slow dance

Romance without love would make me needy
I'd no longer treasure moments alone
I'd be jealous of my partner, greedy
I'd be. Act rash then feel need to atone

But with love I'd be with her when apart
The special bond would keep us together
We would come to know each other by heart
We'd be happy in all kinds of weather

Just two souls happy to have found a match
Romance's itch we would then often scratch

Pick a star

Can we pick a star for our very own
We'll spend lots of time with heads together
Finding dreams to come true, from our hearts grown
And from seeds we newly planted, weather

And time withstanding we'll look at each star
Compare them all, let our hearts argue it
Til they both agree that's the one so far
Away, hope all the other couples quit

Before they reach our star ,we still could share
They could not match our cauliflower ears
Our three eyes sorting and filing with stare
Couldn't keep up with us, they'd be in arrears

We'll know it's neighbors and where it will be
When we're distant we'll look at it with glee

Tandem

If we're on a Tandem bike you should steer
That way I won't be distracted by me
So won't crash turning to speak, you can hear
With me brushing your ear as words flow free

I'd be employed trying not to miss things
You say, Your voice to me is like nature
The wind whistling through the trees, then it sings
Trill of songbirds mixed with the wind for sure

It's the waves dashing to shore over trill
With the wind filling spaces in between
Bees buzzing along side wave's crash, befrill
Round sweet trill with soothing winds all convene

Turns to a chorus of words that you say
I hear them all, no sounds get in their way

"10-01, Girls in glasses day"

I see glasses in Ten Oh One with ease
October first girl's glasses day says bard
Girls with glasses oft like homemade cookies
Lots are vegetarian, in world, card

Greeting's graced girls glamor glasses galore
<I checked, October first is World card Day
Vegetarian, home made cookie> more
Room. I'll add Girls with Glasses anyway

Boys don't make passes at girls with glasses
But I'll give fourteen a white or green rose
If she'd like such a thing when she passes
Free to choose or not to crinkle her nose

So come on guys start the cookies mixing
Through world make a card, veg meal start fixing

Something stuck

Is that something stuck on your shoe, Nice boots
If it's chewing gum must be some old stuff
I think formula was changed by some suits
Now it only sticks to concrete, it's tough

It's not toilet paper, you'd check yourself
Or check to see if someone would tell you
Is it a pixie or a teeny elf
Some guys might think it's their broken-heart blue

But it couldn't be, might step on one's facade
You'd never walk out on a heart sincere
Could be some postage stamps, mail to Belgrade
Or some other foreign spot, seems like here

Might not hold your attention, no fun zones
Oh! Your sole has attracted heart shaped stones

Love dazzles

Like a brave thief you stole my heart by day
Like dreams you will return it in the night
Flying without leaving the field of play
Buying into minutes, no thought of plight

All of the things around us gained beauty
Was the magnificence always around
Did love make a clear view from one sooty
Or rose colored vision seeming profound

Likely the latter, love blinds like the sun
Dazzling our eyes we see things that aren't there
We'll need our hearts to find the way as one
Minefields that could explode our love are there

We'll proceed with feel, sight and hearing lost
You can taste my lips kissing your lips glossed

Kissing

I could feel your knees buckle as we kissed
With our arms firmly about each other
Your sigh of contentment showed you were blissed
As your soft lips moved in for another

Holding you felt like holding a feather
With my eyes closed I heard the flap of wings
I could smell the sweet scent of heather
Thought I heard the sound of symphony strings

Smelled apple blossoms and heard sweet bird's song
Made me know birds had landed on a tree
And my feet were landing on the ground strong
It felt like heaven for you and me

The joys I heard found there could never match
The pleasure I feel hearing your breath catch

Grown rose

Without love no one would have grown a rose
Roses must have been developed long past
Thousands of years to get the right heart glows
Past detractors must of said they won't last

I think history shows the loud hot breeze
Denounce love, don't want a cure for symptoms
They deny having what they call disease
Love grew from warmth's need and to have young'uns

Love and denial of it's existence
Are twins. Neanderthals have a bad rap
Ugly and stupid is the insistence
Some lived decades past limb lost in mishap

Love would keep one alive some think useless
Conquered don't write history, life's a mess

Love in silence

My words are getting in the way of us
We need a date in silence just walking
There would be the oh's and ah's, beauteous
Things we're seeing would replace talking

We'd get good at speaking volumes with looks
There's hundreds of different feelings expressed
By it's own unique smile, such a thing hooks
Our unspoken thoughts together, they're pressed

Like autumn leaves in a book that we chose
I"d find I would not be able to draw
Away from your warm eyes that hold mine froze
As our soft gaze becomes a tether's claw

Who needs words when we have all the world wide
We'll talk if there's future plans to decide

Love in lights

Some love is built in the dark watching lights
Fireworks are a popular thing to see
By a close pair and stars on Cloudless nights
Are just exquisite, moonlight blurs starry

Nights, But it's like gold blurring silver sheen
Nothing is lost, the enchantment does stay
The face of your loved one looking serene
With a warmish glow coming from a blush

Up from their heart as you speak of the glow
In your heart, you see the bright in their eyes
There and in the candlelight that's aglow
In your realm, reminding you of fireflies

On warm nights flitting about in their dance
Of love, thus putting you in a love trance

Hard waiting

It's hard waiting, even those with patience
Are tested, they know it's only time spent
All other occasions had impermanence
Helps for Christmas and Holiday's torment

You can recall how heart tearing waiting
For it's eve, or wishing drop-ins would leave
Knowing it's finite it still is grating
<If from recalling, you'd like a reprieve>

Imagine waiting on indefinite
Time to have your "one" return to your side
The doubts that arise, and fears that alight
Did you show enough caring to turn tide

Or their doubts arise of too much too soon
Hard waiting reveals a passion astrewn

Song of the midst

Like living in a myth whence heroes stem
I feel a strong siren's pull to the curve
Of your lips, and to your eyes, each a gem
The song comes up from my heart with a verve

Obscuring the source, my ears cannot hear
A song of the midst, rather I feel swell
As a stretching of the heart upwards near
My throat, lifting my soul, up I rappel

My core expands to a swell in the chest
Down, my essence, like a glow, will abound
Imbuing all my leg muscles with zest
I feel my feet hardly touching the ground

My very pith raised to dizzying height
The nucleus of my being takes flight

Mackinac love

On Mackinac Island we keep our word
Say we'll be someplace, we won't be absent
Wild horses couldn't keep us away befurled
Now the tame horses that's something different

What Mackinac Island gives she does take
People mix freely love rules don't apply
No enclosures except the ones folks make
To show they're out of the game, love's nearby

When needed, complete with quaint surroundings
Beauty fills your eyes being by the lake
When translucent green waves pull on heartstrings
Walking down wooded trails, for touch you ache

But it is love in an incubator
With much there to act as agitator

Stolen time

Not enough hours in the day for romance
We'll get stolen kisses with borrowed time
With our backs against the wall we will dance
Nose to the grindstone we'll stop on a dime

Completely. So we may get nine cents change
We will put in our two cents and for thought
We'll have plenty penny, midnight oil range
To sunrise, minding our own beeswax bought

With earned penny saved, we'll use all the time
In the middle when burning the candle
At both ends, push the hands on clock sublime
We'll spend time together til' a handle

The world gets and catches up with us, now
We'll find the time to enjoy love and how

Your Texting

Your nimble fingers dream waltz on the keys
Sending your well-considered opinions
Holding nothing back, each line is not tease
You give completely to all your minions

Providing a banquet of food for thought
It's all organically grown in mind
Providing nourishment that has been sought
By the reader's heart that's seeking to find

Strength transferred with honest words being sent
Daily requirement gets to the reader
No deficiency, not even a dent
The truth will be present at the feeder

Spreading out over the land all around
Gets into people's mind without a sound

No regrets

You have a joy for life don't want regrets
Follow your heart places it goes deterred
By nothing, standing fast ignoring threats
To your happiness heart sends love outward

The world cannot get you down, hands on hips
"How dare they try" Said with defiance firm
But still it's spoke with a smile on your lips
Troubles pass, your belief it does affirm

Serendipity is brought from bad luck
Gets easier to salvage good from bad
It's an acquired talent, life goes amuck
Is a fact, can't live life shielded by sad

Could scare happiness away with a frown
Your frown is nice, it's installed upside down

Hey buddy

Hey buddy! I'd say I miss you but can't
I have my feelings for you in my heart
In my mind I have memories you plant
When you recall things that makes you laugh, start

A smile that ends at my toes, your soft face
I picture in my mind all through the light
In the dark it deserts me <it's with grace>
You're a friend in the day not of the night

The important thing is that you get me
I don't even explain myself too well
Just don't feel I am confused in your mind
You've figured me out right away, that's swell

All that I know is here, nothing to miss
That could change should we ever share a kiss

Making love

It seems to many people making love
Is a journey's end before beginning
On a new journey. I've found from above
An angel in you, we will be winning

<Tie for first> If we make love to refuel
The love we made in our hearts and our minds
I feel we have reached what only a few
Ever do, an intimacy that binds

Us in a journey together, a touch
Was all it took for us to get started
A smell put us in a spell very much
Our eyes showed us we would be true-hearted

As we were lost in an easy locked gaze
I've learned our tastes are alike in past days

Busy thinking

I think pass yourself when thinking of you
I start thinking of all the stunning things
I have seen and sharing them, with us two
Finding exquisite things seen shared, it brings

Two closer, I think of where things stunning
Spring from, beautiful mountain stream falling
Over rocks, sends the sad feelings running
The snow melt and falling rain come calling

Gorgeous blooms with mix of orange and yellow
On same flower, from pollen off a bee
Stunning mountain views I recall, mellow
Out my feelings, knowing heights reached will be

Done over time, all the wonders of earth
Like our feelings at sometime had a birth

Our Plenary Love

Outbreaks of opportunity open
Up, unsung unwed us, umbra unseen
Ruthlessly request restless regimen

Passion pairs proliferate, preen pristine
Little love lent lights lover's lasting loop
Existing eternally excepting
Negation, name not needy Nincompoop
Always abide all, also accepting
Rambling relativity runs random range
Your yummy yowl yanks yonder, yielding yet

Looming love large. Listen, lyrical lute
Orchestrating Orchid odor's onset
Valued vanguard vanquish vapid vista
Exit every ear, enter eclat

A Purple Passion

Apologies are antiquated

Purple powers prove proper poise precise
Undertone unrestrained, unabated
Reaches "rareair" relaxing, restrains rice
Positivity pads possible pain
Living life large, lack lackadaisical
Efforts, enthusiasm entertain

Passion panchromatic poetical
Answers arising anonymously
Showing some sticky situations solved
Shade Satin shining synonymously
In issues, intrigue, inhabit involved
Only open ones occupy oneness
Noble nearness needed now nonetheless

Skidoodle

Sometimes I see you coming down the street
I have a whelming urge to skidoodle
My feelings for you overwhelm my feet
And patterns in the soft earth I doodle

Think it's fear of surrendering to you
Which means I am not using my noodle
Not sharing my heart is making me blue
You are the one I want to skidoodle

To a private place with us as a pair
The love I feel for you is an oodle
It permeates widespread breathable air
And makes all my old sadness skidoodle

I will continue to fight this strong urge
To flee, so our lives can finally merge

Boing!

When you first wake up in the early morn
Is it with a Boing? That's the sound I hear
Before my alarm goes off with it's horn
I turn it off and pop up if day's clear

It's with a boing eager to face a day
That all of my dreams may start to come true
Do you sit up with a boing feeling gay
From glad dreams. Boings are inspired by you

Not so much from your looks, beauty you own
Classic with a touch of exotica
But the personality you have grown
Seems to align well with mine, trivia

You recall makes me sit up and listen
What you believe in makes my heart glisten

◦~◦

Kindred souls

Two kindred souls had met at a crossroads
They then went on together as a pair
There was no question asked of which road holds
Their shared destiny neither had to wear

The other down to be the boss, each leg
Went the same way, was that the way that fate
Had meant it, part of a plan, does fate egg
Peoples lives along. Or was it each gait

Was on the same path alone, together
Now, they'll continue on that trail, new life
Built frompast experiences leather
Will weather tides, building a strong heart, strife

Continues on down the road not taken
Their meeting caused two hearts to awaken

Tilt

I tilt at rainbows, call me Quixotic
Windmills are just not allowed around here
I look for a chance to be heroic
Making up for people's shortcomings dear

Sacrificing my heart going along
With the tide when it's the right thing to do
Appearing weak to make others feel strong
I'll fight the current to give one their due

I am carrying a double-edged sword
Forged by heartaches, one edge cuts pain from life
But one edge stops feelings being explored
With the people who could save me from strife

I might just work myself into a lave
Fighting rainbows for the magic they have

Hope

All my life I've heard in stories and song
About people with the world in their hand
No stress, troubles or worries come along
But yet they are bored their life seems so bland

People struggling to get along wonder
Just how anyone could believe such lies
Tears truth in media all asunder
Think deeply it will come as no surprise

Hope could be the most valuable thing
That can be found in the world by someone
It can be had by those who have nothing
But those with everything may have none

Still I wish all could have their dreams fulfilled
And not be bored, prove me wrong, I'd be thrilled

Small world

We meet again, didn't expect to see you
Traveling in quirky circles, must be
Destined to cross paths, til they merge anew
Do our peculiar quirks we don't see

Direct our movements through life's staunch gauntlets
Cause us to be in the same time and place
Repeatedly through our lives like jaunt pets
These same quirks make us require breathing space

Many get annoyed by quirks of their friends
Not accepting they have quirks of their own
Those quirks are by-products, not dividends
Of the personalities that we've grown

By instinct chosen friends are similar
Would be nice to accept friends as they are

Redundancy

Redundancy can be a form of art
Bad if done wrong, loses relevancy
Accordancy must be kept from the start
You can do it all with vigilancy

Verdancy is acceptable excuse
Used twice it's just an extravagancy
Stagnancy, arrogancy will produce
Those who won't learn should stick with truancy

Exuberancy is a media
That can be used well with elegancy
Fancy a mind's encyclopedia
That will help fight off irrelevancy

Consistancy seeds in me poignancy
Vacancy of heart seeds irritancy

Smiles

I find a smile is always on my mind
In there a smile or two stacked in a pile
I have said it always pays to be kind
You're likely to get paid back with a smile

I would joke that a smile can stop the rain
Also rain fears those who are not afraid
Letting the rain change my plans causes pain
At that time a smile will come to my aid

I know some must smile as part of their job
Their smile sure must be wore down by day's end
A smile can be handy when you hob-nob
Or you could save your smile for a close friend

Even if you were to not smile all day
You could still be happy in your own way

Guardian angel

Didn't believe in Angels til' my hopes sagged
And I stopped caring what I ever did
But then I saw you and all my doubts lagged
Recalled a promise I made, I wouldn't kid

Stopped me from doing things I would regret
Thought you could be my guardian angel
But you have not flown off to heaven yet
Perhaps you can stay but I won't compel

Use your wings so to be free as a bird
Hover about me to save me from harm
If you should feel like being good-natured
Like a falcon you can rest on my arm

If I don't make an effort to believe
But I do, that thing is real, I perceive

Enthusiastically smiling (Part 1)

I Owe you two hundred smiles, I reckon
If I'd weigh them, they're from you by the ton
A grin, beam a silly ear-to-ear grin
Favor me with a goofy one, no sin

Your promiscuous smile, it's heavenly
It is like the blessed smile of a baby
Waking up to see mom, that is profound
Easy smile is that of a lazy hound

Mighty is your Mona Lisa smile, sweet
Is smile of affirmation, that is neat
Pleased like the cat who ate the canary
Or maybe it's extraordinary

Like a great big canary ate the cat,
Canary pleased as punch, crazy as that
I do like your familiar brainy smile
It's weatherproof and fireproof all the while

Enthusiastically smiling (Part 2)

Your memorable Cheshire grin is charmed
Life of the party, <was not a smile harmed
In the making of this poem. Sincere!>
Dreamed for days of your laconic smile, dear

Though it's disjointed, I am not perplexed
Your strong heroic face muscles are all flexed
I adore a heartfelt smile that's bombproof
And unless I'm confused it's waterproof,

It's not soaked in tears, slightly impressive
I don't get scared at smile introspective
Not afraid to show your smile fool-hardy
You trust my virtuous smile, we'll party

Restrained, but be assured, serious fun
Will be had. Giddy before we are done.
Never seems polished, but relaxed and real
I see your spry smile, warm-hearted I feel

Enthusiastically smiling (Part 3)

Your perceptive smile of understanding
Is irrepressibly non-demanding
I've seen smile diminutive and not so
Smile capacious, with your face aglow

Smile toothsome, lights the night so radiant
Smile unguarded and full-blown, resplendent.
Furtive when you're being mysterious
That's persuasive when you're impetuous

Mesmerizing is your eccentric grin
Authoritative you are when lips thin
Idiosyncratic you is gripping
When you're disheveled my heart is skipping

Your healing smile is showing you're steadfast
That's refreshing and something that will last
It's encouraging to a trusting soul
That's gratifying like your ardentwhole

Enthusiastically smiling (Part 4)

Unfading unapologetical
For the prolific intellectual
Not just curious, but adventurous
Your hyena grin is more then precious

Fanciful smile is hopeful and pearly
Poised and devoted, won't give up early
Uplifted dreams soothing and enchanting
I'm aware, gentle feelings it's planting

Altruistic dotings inspired quick
By tender exuberance, but they'll stick
Shown joyful and thoughtful concern is pure
Tender meaningful smile is your allure

Your complimentary smile is telling
My boyish and hellish grin is selling
The fun behind my manly smile flashing
I'll flatter with chivalrous smile dashing

Enthusiastically smiling (Part 5)

Does not feel foolish or childish, your proud
Smile stirs my urge to divide from the crowd
Tenderly, your fabulous smile brings forth
Generous feelings of robust self-worth

Stirring up enigmatic dreams of old
Times that were winsome lonesome, thoughts were bold
Actions were weak, smile chaste was all I'd see
Had a keen earnest, worldly-wise to be

So willful and indefatigable
But still eager to remain laudable
Spirited, more bemused then irked, helpful
But not forward, zealous to be cheerful

Wistful and naïve, wanting to keep mild
Remain conscientious to hide the wild
To try hard to be humble seemed clever
Stay innocent, lose childlike charm never

Enthusiastically smiling (Part 6)

Wouldn't be shrewd, self-consciously I'd feel
An unnatural fixed smile wouldn't appeal
Still smile amenable and concordant
Would be there, matter of fact it's poignant

A Faint smile would be on my face briefly
Innocuous smile would be used chiefly
It would be too sublime and whimsical
I'd become. Smile subtle and lyrical

May not show you my boisterous nature
I'd show hardy and healthy smile for sure
Your warm self-assured way is genial
With a smile casual and cordial

Up from your heart with an exquisite shine
Wholesome and delightfully genuine
Your demeanor is glib, but erudite
Still with a smile congenial and bright

Enthusiastically smiling (Part 7)

To show you're pleasantly intelligent
Alert, wise, dignified and confident
I esteem your smile attractive and plucky
It's irresistible, makes me sappy
Lavish me with your matchless graceful smile
And spectacularly dynamic style
Is my own stupendous golden secret
Elegant is your smile soft and quiet

Profuse is your smile florid and honeyed
Richly delicate. Beats being moneyed
Like the smile watching humming bird hover
Many smiles left for us to discover

On stage

Ad lib theater troupes are like the sunsets
There are nights some don't go on, beauty waits
Backstage for chance to face foot light's assets
Purple anxious for her turn, needs more dates

Not been out for weeks, she's in the background
Her over whelming beauty elbowed out
By yellows and oranges that abound
Wisp of a cloud enters the scene, no doubt

Red follows close behind, Oh! Look who's here.
Purple has come out and she's everywhere
Flits from red to yellow to orange with cheer
Then she seems to become part of the air

Leaving bits behind to fade like the day
Like the set sun purple has gone away

Lift up

Ever feel blue and don't know what to do
You tried being rude so to get it out
Failed. Here's a trick I learned when I was two
You can find ways to lend a helping hand

Don't think that's too easy to have value
After all saying "God bless you" to sneeze
Works to lift your smile, sneeze ain't always due
Don't carry pepper to induce it, please

Picking up some loose trash makes me feel good
Don't think how it got there, it needs picking
You might feel better, you know if you would
Smile at sad people their wounds need licking

Make yourself feel better on the double
Just help someone get over their trouble

Perspective

Camping at the creek, look up from your fire
You will see a log cabin way up there
On the mountain top, a cabin for hire
Renters look out to see the city air

With lights seeming to float above the ground
Man in a penthouse apartment looks out
To navy blue sea where life does abound
Sees the lights of a ship, it's just about

To fade from view, most of those on the ship
Look forward, that's where there life is found at
Others leave behind a relationship
Some look back in regret others stand pat

They are watching because in the city
Their loved ones watch them get itty-bitty

∽

Uniqueness of purple

The uniqueness of purple earns it friends
It has many traits that set it apart
But a few of it's traits fit other trends
Like orange and silver you can't impart

A rhyme on it. It's name lent to rare things
Purple bacteria makes energy
Through photosynthesis a new life springs
When in state and at an academy

Purple does represent a high standard
In people it represents good judgment
And the quest for inner peace, meandered
Souls find repose in purple, discontent

Of red<mad> and blue<sad> heals by magic
When combined in purple, holds life's fabric

Flowers for a Purple Wedding (Part 1)

Much meaning has been assigned to flowers
None so much as Purple ones, Dahlia
Stands for gratitude, Aster empowers
With elegance, you find in Freesia

Innocence, which fits with Lilac's first Loves
Hope fortune of Cornflower brought friendship
With Rose's enchantment, love's first sight shoves
The Anemone in your hand with grip

Of anticipation, Tulips passion
Mixes with laughs and open heartedness
Of Larkspur, Calla lily in fashion
With it's beauty, it's not just for deadness

Flowers for a Purple Wedding (Part 2)

Be attracted to meaning of Iris
Wisdom and eloquence, the Charisma
Of Lisianthus is a good virus
To catch with congeniality's rah!

Ochid's rare beauty can't match Violet's
Faithfulness teamed with modesty. The luck
Of Lavender shall be with you, beget
Gladiolus generosity, Pluck

Sweetpeas for blissful pleasure, feel airy
With Delpiniums, Hydrageas bring
Devotion and understanding very
Friendly, the Hyacinths have the gold ring

℘

Ambrosia's day (Part 1)

Ambrosia sits in her parlour, set
To return love, as friends, loves and other
Pay call, she dreams of Red Rose, true love met.
But thinks of Forget-Me-Not, another

Kept secret, but Acacia's love shows.
Art dealer Acanthus drops in, hater
Aconite comes with. Agrimony knows
Girl's proud he comforts Aloe's grief state, her

Promise is in Almond, Amaranth gives
Her hope there's forever love. Trefoil grudged
But Star of Bethlehem there and forgives.
Hermit Lichen makes rare stop, Ivy trudged

A long way to pay visit, Blue Rose strives
To win with mystery, Balm soothes Oak Leaf's
Worked muscles. Amaryllis pride brings hives.
Docile Bulrush will heal Black Rose griefs

Ambrosia's day (Part 2)

Royal Angrec , Apple Blossoms prefer
Life friend Arborvitae's date, Arbutus
Loves only her, dainty charm of Aster
Hooked Bachelor Button, Hibiscus

Is a rare and delicate friend, Arum
Born with look of ardor, Fascination
Asparagus provides. Asphadel glum
His regrets stay to death. Red Carnation

Has aching heart from Striped's love refusal
Red's White love has turned Yellow, but Mom's Pink
Comforts him, Mauve turns him to perusal
Of fantasy dreams. Azalea thinks

Baby's Breath innocence and purity
Should be preserved, Balsam's love is fervent
Balsamine Impatiens, Bay Wreath's glory
Hunger to be like noble Thistle, pent

Ambrosia's day (Part 3)

Dreams must end, though like Berrirose, she'll stick
By, constant like Box, Begonia has charmed
Bellflower but should beware, she will flick
From crush to crush, Ireland Bells be not harmed

With luck, Birds of Paradise perspective
Makes them magnificently free, chestnut
Says "do right" Humble Broom will learn to live
Coriander, Lime Blossom, stuff they'll strut

Bumblebee Orchid works hard, Buttercup
Likes cabbage for his profit. No false tells
Camellia Japonica chin up
Campanula and Canterbury Bells

Ring out in Gratitude, Cherry Blossom
Well taught, Celandine knows of future joy
China Aster loves Red Chrysanthemum
Who feels loving thoughts of things to enjoy

Ambrosia's day (Part 4)

Yellow has no joyful thoughts, feels slighted
Coreopsis and Cowslip live with grace
Red Clover works hard, White could be knighted
Delphinium master of time and space

Doubtful Daffodil's unrequited love
Springs from chivalry, despair of Cypress
Fits sorrow over loss of mourning dove
Elegant Dahlia, Daisies impress

With loyal simple well-thought out love, Red
Beauty sees one mirror, Honeysuckle's
Eyes. Him and sis Heliotrope wellbred
Gorse knows no season without love, chuckles

For Roses, red and yellow together
All the emotions of love bad and good
Of yellow, finds red bird of a feather
Light pink and coral find passion withstood

Ambrosia's day (Part 5)

Through time. The pink and dark roses thankful
For burgundies unknown beauty. White rose
With a green tint I'm pleased to bring, heart full
Strong flatterer I am, some deceit grows

Eglantine Rose relates with unhealed wound
I fade out to observe, Elderflower
I hold for compassion, feelings attuned
Dear Plumeria hosts baby shower

In Fungus I see me, a tough hermit,
We're just glad Gardenia exists, Housesleek
Fungus leaves with posh Geranium, Brit
Hollyhock's ambition fits grass who's meek

Rue regrets not returning Jonquil's warmth
Laurestine presents Mallow, he's consumed
Around Laurel, who's a star, Lilacs swarmth
Morning Glory's Love Lies Bleeding assumed

Ambrosia's day (Part 6)

Cold hearted lettuce may melt from trusting
Lily Of The Valley, cause she's demure
Lemon Blossom is prudent, adjusting
With the thrift of Thyme, Magnolia lure

Of nature with good Mullein, now Lily
Pure White, proud Scarlet and warm Orange call
Mints misgivings pain Marigold, silly!
They'd match with Peach Bloom's hopes of a long haul

Poor well-spoken chaste Lotus, malevent
Lobelia lures, Mayflower welcome
With worthy Mignonette, Moonflowers bent
On love dreams, hero Nasturtium become

Friends with Olive through Oat's music, Orchid
The beauty shined accepts Viscaria
Witch-Hazel sends winged seeds as they dance, bid
Of love wins out, courage of Protea

Ambrosia's day (Part 7)

Primes long love in Primrose, Blossom Of Plum
She is, everlasting beauty she holds
Phlox soul harmonized with Pitchpine Blossom
Philosophies match, Oxeye Daisy molds
Patience in Creeping Willow, who's lovelorn
Bashful Peony close, shame to not speak
All poppies dream of hope, some dreams sleep torn
The hostess and Rosemary recall peak

Days of youth, Tulip's love is undying
Yellow's is hopeless. Truth is bittersweet
Thorn apple incognito, he's lying
To pure Sunflower with false dreams offbeat

Well named Sensitive Plant feels Snowdrop's hopes
For comfort. Straw and pure sweetbriar are one
Tulip tree with fame meets Wheat's wealth, no mopes
Violets true blue, Ambrosia is done

Flowers play (Part 1)

I did see the show in question last night
This reviewer forgot about the plot
Caught up in the characters and their plight
On top of that the work's name I forgot

Fell asleep planning gardens, wild and tame
Dreamed for what felt like hours of flowers play
I meant to write my review, just the same
As always, after planning for next May

But I woke up with a lap full of books
All I can do now is write of the dream
Least what I can dredge out of my brain's nooks
My dream opened with a drawn curtain, beam

Of light shining on Crocus with foresight
Rhododendron next appears says beware
Do not presume, like Snapdragon, lore might
Turn out like many others, be aware

Flowers play (Part 2)

With enthusiasm of Day Lily
And peacefulness of Cosmo, of hidden
Nuances like Holly acting silly
From domestic happiness, doubt ridden

Out of her mind by Pansy's loving thought
Steadfast Wisteria likes Queen Anne's lace
Delicate femininity but caught
By Ranunculus and her beaming face

Solitude of Heather, indecision
Has bred, Gladiolus gives him the strength
Of character to know inclination
Towards standing fast by his choice at length

Is in him. Black-eyed Susan gives her friend
The aspiring Astroemeria
Encouragement, Statice wishes no end
Of her success, Lily Casablanca

Flowers play (Part 3)

Hosts a celebration for Stargazer
Who's chasing her ambition with Yarrow
Who supports good health, and with proud Ginger
Opened a fertility clinic, go

With the name Orange Blossom, dear Jasmine
Suggests with grace and elegance. Bonne chance
Says Steplantotis. Zinnia has fine
Thoughts of friends, doting Sunflower who once

Saw Tuberose and fell in love, pleasure
Was there with the Passion flower's treasure

Pillow talk

I like feather pillows more then foam ones
Though I had a stiff foam pillow I'd use
Made a great armless husband <any puns?>
But then before long stiffness it would lose

And become perfect for my head to rest
Was a sure winner in a pillow fight
To get it broken in is a good quest
Can not fluff it up to get feathers light

And you will not get poked by feather's shaft
Or get soaked by paying ten times as much
For a Down pillow that can't be a raft
Still to me nothing beats the touch

Of Down surrounding feathers on my crown
Beware! Foam pillows on sale are "Marked Down"

Flying time

If you time the minutes as they go by
You'd be surprised to learn they're all the same
Been said and you know it's true, time will fly
That does apply when life is a fun game

We push the clock through times we must endure
Nothing stops it from gaining momentum
All the best minutes go by in a blur
Many folks still have times they feel humdrum

Good times need brakes so as to slow them down
Break off bits of good times, mix with the slow
Just could be boredom is caused by a frown
Caught in the time stream to interrupt flow

Don't lose the good times in boredom or strife
Do your best to keep control of your life

Gently slid

You gently slid into my heart, freeing
Me from the prison of walls I have built
I feel you've absorbed my very being
Making me feel whole and removing guilt

Brought upon me when trying to find love
Knowing now those ones were just a bad fit
Just like putting on a four-fingered glove
Ignoring the fact it wouldn't fit my mitt

Being blind to any obvious sign
Because of overwhelming need to pair
And being drawn to someone who looks fine
Just because that's the person that is there

With the talent to sensationalize
Now with you the past seems a blest disguise

Life of an arrow

Are you living your life like an arrow
That's been shot by an archer from a bow
Do your choices in life all seem narrow
As if you are stuck on a path aglow

Guideposts along the way to mark a trail
Steer you on by senses, a siren sings
Your nose sweet and spicy smells will assail
There's many seemingly familiar things

You just keep moving on as if compelled
Having no doubt about decisions made
Seems by some unknown force you are propelled
Arrows that hit their mark have never strayed

The archer's aim was true blue from the start
Their keenness of eye came right from the heart

No lonely moon

Moon does not look lonely though it's alone
It does reflect the warm light of the sun
But there's been no one around while it shone
It exists with purpose, knows not love's fun

Many people are like that, just exist
Others depend on them to be a rock
Like the moon if they were gone they'd be missed
No one has turned their heart key to unlock

Their existence is denied in the night
Once the day is through they become unseen
If one thought to ask them to the moonlight
May decide it's not part of their routine

It's like showing someone a daytime moon
They won't look at it, they say it's too soon

The thought becomes the gift

Thought is all that counts when giving a gift
Seems to me the thought becomes the present
That token gives receivers heart a lift
They want to display it like a crescent

So all the world can see they are loved
Jewelry seems wasted cash to a man
But hand wearing gifted ring won't be gloved
Gift necklace will be worn against her tan

To enhance the beauty her love holds dear
Flowers, candy and liquor are all fine
But they will all be gone too soon I fear
Give an everlasting gift while you dine

So it will show to her how much you care
And that you think of her when she's not there

"Missed Maybes"

Of it's beauty the Island is bereft
I no longer hear the songbirds singing
It seems to have been like this since you left
Are they seeking you, I see them winging

All the folks I see have empty faces
I search them all, I'm looking for your smile
None I see I'd want their lip gloss traces
I'd be glad to find a Bibliophile

Books are my only solace, flowers bright
In them. Around me flowers seem washed out
I've seen no baby ducks out in the light
Only broken shells, makes me want to pout

Thoughts of mom crying about lost babies
Just like I'm crying over missed maybes

Waiting for Rainbows

At the end of a rainbow can be found
A pot of gold just waiting to be grabbed
The myth, trail one end to gold, is renowned
If it's not there it's already been nabbed

Keep searching on, do not give up your dreams
There will always be another rainbow
You can enjoy the days of sunlight's beams
Gone are rainy days you felt the pain grow

Waiting for rainbows will give you a lift
Follow them and all those dreams which linger
Dread the days no longer, live each day's gift
The world will be wrapped around your finger

Binds will lift from your heart and you'll feel free
Life becomes the joy it was meant to be

Poet not a lover

I am just a poet not a lover
I feel like love is just one of the arts
When romance comes calling I take cover
I'm too fickle, I don't want to break hearts

What if I make a promise to a girl
Then meet one who I think is my soul mate
And in her hair is a cute little curl
Would I stick by the first cause she's my fate?

All I know about love is from stories
Songs, poems and some psalms that I have read
Know about love's defeats and it's glories
I Do not know what it's like to be wed

Loving looks and caresses I have missed
I have forgot what it's like to be kissed

Are you a Princess?

Are you a Princess? It seems so to me
You are charming in the way you treat folks
Never belittle anyone you see
No one but you are the butt of your jokes

You're not lifted up by putting folks down
It seems like you never have a bad day
Whatever goes wrong you don't show your frown
Overcoming struggles seems like child's play

Each opportunity you make the best
You pull yourself up by your own shoestrings
Only thing given to you is a quest
As if it's a mission given by kings

Not bitter. Seems you've never had a woe
Entitlement is not something you show

Important poets

Can poets be considered important
They do not save lives like a fireman would
Thoughts they convey are not unimportant
They give folks reasons for living, that's good

Poems sent to kindred spirits by them
That can do a world of good in rough times
Let the lonely know that they are a gem
Each and every one will shine sometimes

They don't improve your health like doctors might
But poets can put a lift in your heart
And a bounce in your stride so you step light
World changes with help of the poet's art

May point out wrongs that could be corrected
Helps human consciousness stay connected

Sonneteer

Dictionary defines a Sonneteer
One who writes inferior poetry
It seems they have an ax to grind I fear
They sure show "The Bard" no civility

"What thou sayeth ?" he may think if he could
As for me I pull for the underdog
To me a fourteen line poem looks good
Fourteen strokes I count when sawing a log

I then take a rest and count fourteen more
Seven is lucky, fourteen is twice that
I hope I am not becoming a bore
A sonneteer writes a sonnet, that rat

Certainly would not want to leave that out
After all that is what this is about

Poet Hotline

Forgot anniversary or birthday
And a six-pack won't cut it anymore
Call our poet hotline, do it today
Spice up the wilted bouquet from the store

If your lady's love has turned into hate
Custom poems in your hand in an hour
Get a personal poem while you wait
Just maybe I should say while you cower

And always on special is a Sonnet
We can't give same day service on that one
Our Sonnet writer is a poor poet
We'll send you that poem when it is done

Our poets have master English degrees
We recruit from the fast food industries

Poetry Police

I heard you recite as I was leaving
May I see you poetic license please
Iambic pentameter is weaving
You're dropping the's and I's with too much ease

Your sentence structure is against the rules
Too many of your poems seem the same
Do you think readers are a bunch of fools
All your puns are unbelievably lame

Wait while I write your license number down
I need to look over this license too
It's not duly authorized for this town
Powers that be won't let me ticket you

I'd warn you but you wouldn't listen I fear
So I'm telling you just get out of here

Writer's block

I'm not feeling very poetic now
Fore' I wrote poems used to feel that way
When younger I'd have the urge and allow
Myself to talk in rhymes most any day

But I was just a kid of forty-eight
Just one poem had I written by then
Soon wrote thoughts down, when forgot that's too late
Mixed with recurring thoughts, stirred with a pen

Often think in a ten-syllable line
For the most part didn't use a rhyming guide
The first hundred I'd rack that brain of mine
But repetition is undignified

With all my thoughts on paper my mind's clear
Soon my poetic thoughts will reappear

Poets Bleah!

These poems should be written, said the man
On some squeezably soft paper for use
He didn't mean a pillow for his divan
Do poets deserve a heap of abuse

Well I for one always thought that they did
Could have written pulp mystery novels
Or spy books, I didn't mind if we could rid
The world of poets in filthy hovels

Read about their lives they're mostly deranged
Does that sound like anyone that you know
Who needs poems they are just words arranged
But animals like the rhythm, girls glow

Things that reduce ladies stress can't be bad
But now stop me before I rhyme again

Filthy Hovels

Filthy hovels is the stereotype
That poets have fallen under I feel
I think it's reality and not hype
Hard to think poetic under some heel

Got to get away from control to write
So that you can be undisturbed to think
Someplace dim, muse won't come if it's too bright
To keep folks from staying, maybe a stink

Not too much just some incense can repel
If that's your thing, clear out those who are loud
Don't think a muse likes hearing someone yell
Certainly can't write poems in a crowd

While writing this my eye's gotten a tick
To scare people off that will do the trick

Scrape

Ask why I write poetry, I might say
The grime of living off my soul, I'll scrape
So it can shine once again, and it may
Reflect into my heart, and not escape,

That which is all about, the good feelings
Coming from those around and to deflect
Bad feelings, that I get in my dealings
From those with false pride, who try to affect

The true pride which I own, they'd like to quash
To lift themselves by putting others down
Never works, it all comes out in the wash
Of the poems cleansing, to clear a frown

Which just may otherwise replace my smile
That could free people from their daily trial

Unflowered

When I looked at an incomplete poem
It was happy to see me, up it perked
Would like to have a flower on it's stem
Tired of sitting, show it my pen still worked

It knows I have more to say about it
But I still think it needs to rest a while
I think it needs to cure and age a bit
I'm worried, if hurried, I'll change it's style

Don't recall having this much fun with pen
Leastways not since I was five with crayon
And coloring books from the five and ten
Outside the lines, that can be relied on

Fore' I break them all, I'll get "list of rules"
I'll kick the words round, scrape them off my shoes

Eyes looking out

As a photographer studies a shot
Making sure all is in focus, good light
Proper subject position and what not
Artist makes sure the still life is just right

A poet gets their subject down pat too
Gentle nuances must be understood
See motivation behind what they do
See through another's eyes as if they could

Artists and photographers self-portray
Most poems deal with how the poet feels
Reactions to sensations in their way
Opens up their hearts and shows us their zeal

Photogs and artists have their tools about
Poets stand around with eyes looking out

Bouncer

When I write poetry, I send it out
It's like a child leaving home to belong
And the world will decide what they're about
Could be a story or changed to a song

What it is about, your feelings decide
I write each line to rhyme with it's cohort
And fit with line before, thoughts start to slide
If tried to send a point, might come up short

Sometimes I have a thought that runs right through
Slow down to avoid rhyming conundrums
With some words, you don't know, trouble could brew
Need a bouncer for poems, keep out bums

My muse does not like words that cause trouble
Grab their neck, kick them out on the double

Words

In the dictionary, a word that's good
"Quay" it's a solid landing place for ships
Implies a harbor, against storms it stood
"Foundation to anchor to", like friendships

That's a poetic thought, wide use it lacks
Many seemingly useful words don't last
So what happened, did they fall through the cracks
Did they get blown away by the wind's blast

Betimes is another, it means early
People like different names for the same thing
Seems it would get used, sounds too quaint surely
Quaint; quirky and odd, that's how I'm thinking

Words like all other things go out of style
But like style, not all come back after a while

Anti-poetry

Anti-poetry is what poets write
To balance out the stuff they've had to read
Whether in class or even here. Delight
Is not always found in poems, indeed

Might be was a poem of old days past
Or about future dreams their's to behold
May have been the overdone theme broadcast
Or the hideous style employed so bold

But that poem just rubbed them the wrong way
Might have happened when they were only five
Or twenty five or older but one day
They were fed up, their muse became alive

Could do better than that they decided
To anti-poetry they were guided

Dictionary

This is me, writing a poem standing
Wanted a new one now nothing day old
Hope it works out, don't want a hard landing
Should be easy I'll just follow a mold

No dictionary round, almost can spell
I just consult the town dictionary
When there's a word's meaning I may know well
Just ask an acquaintance who may tarry

They may feel the need to raise a protest
But I try to nudge them gently, I know
About self-doubts, they may feel it's a test
By chance most have the answer as to show

That there is so much knowledge to be found
If you will just ask the people around

Picture poem

It's said a picture paints a thousand words
Just how many words to write a picture
Working that one out are poets in herds
Try to make their scene strong fearing stricture

Should I write a poem like an artist
Painting a picture, I would start with shade
Putting in shadows would seem the smartest
Place to begin, point them correctly. Strayed

Shadows are not what I'm after. Presage
Done, I then would put in the scene's background
Mind the shadow's edge to send the message
Fill in the shadow's shaper all around

Then lastly tie it up not forgetting
To fill the blanks to complete the setting

Rules

Rules can be stopgaps or ways to get out
Depends. A stopgap was what grammar was
To me until I started writing out
My own poetic leanings all abuzz

I thought grammar was there for one reason
Just perpetuating a caste system
That's what I heard folks do, <is this treason?>
Poetic License says "Rules, ignore them"

And I do like to fly without the rules
But when counting syllables I did find
A need to be succinct, found using tools
Of grammar saves from repetition's grind

I discovered Grammar's less pedantic
Then always thought, helps me be romantic

Subconscious

Searching in my notes for a poem new
I leafed right by it thinking it was old
It fit in so well with old poems too
Wrote it day before, was not even cold

It's like reading books that seems familiar
Some passages you know you've read before
Would have been more than half you're life so far
Since this book you have read, can't recall more

This happens in human interactions
I can recall going through the same thing
Know what's next in certain situations
Thoughts sit there in my subconscious waiting

Is it a psychic sub-conscious network
Listening to your heart, this, is a perk

Affectation of Sadness

You need not worry about my sadness
Just an affectation, like a mustache
A mustache hides a lip, I hide gladness
Hide the glad or it will run out like cash

I see people try to hide a feeling
I hide glad, folks in a situation
Show dislike though they find it appealing
Safe to hide behind an affectation

When a person gets overwhelmed by stress
They feel they can lash out at those around
Attitude's an affectation I guess
Does that reveal a judgment that's not sound

I'll watch else the actor becomes the act
Caught up in behavior not hard, that's fact

Difficulties

Can you please stand by temporarily
We have just lost our poetry network
We're having technical difficulty
More than likely it's just a little quirk

Our poet misplaced his sense of wonder
So no poetry until that is found
When a kid, find a log just look under
You would find something there that will astound

For kids wonder's caused by things curious
Adults wonder at curious events
That mess their lives and make them furious
Caused by people and by the governments

That will easily distract anyone
Poets aren't immune save their sense of fun

Quirky and Odd

We've heard that dictionaries don't have ain't
It's there, they just advise against it's use
It's an example of a word that's quaint
I enjoy such things I have a quaint muse

My poetry can be quaint by design
I'd think it's certainly more fun that way
Quirky and odd with me seems to align
With the thoughts and words I'm trying to say

I do have feelings I want to express
Easier being vague and not too clear
Brings out the issues I'd like to address
Print what I feel without boring your ear

Not being yourself, that's quirky and odd
So be soft or hard, spendthrift or tightwad

Emptiness

Drops torn from my eyes by my broken heart
Hitting the parched ground about my two feet
Lays bare what's beneath my eyes torn apart
The broken heart continuing to beat

Is nothing but a pump making blood flow
Out of a heart with no remaining soul
Nothing left there but a puddle of woe
The pain of loss is exacting a toll

Darkness descends on my very being
I'm reliving the sorrow of the loss
All my hopes and dreams of love are fleeing
Each one has turned into nothing but dross

Nothing left but the dwindling of the days
The future I see is nothing but haze

Emotional Expression

Emotional expressions are widespread
Some have a narrow range, frown has one use
That's to indicate a feeling of dread
A smile though could be sad, that's like a bruise

Wistful thoughts of a once upon happy
A sigh rides the entire range of feeling
Could be like slamming doors <if it's snappy>
Expression of "could have", sends you reeling

Indicates frustration as it's main job
Sigh of contentment is exact reverse
Then there's the one when you feel your heart throb
That's when you see your dreamboat, woes disperse

Dreamy sigh holds hopes of solidarity
It is a sigh of prosperity

Spring Break

Shining sun simmers seaside sandy shores
Bikinied brunettes basking by bronzed blonde
Big brutes, bachelor boys becoming bores
Flinging footballs following fillies fond

Telling tales to titillate those tender
Hairless hopeful harlequin hunks hover
Vapid Valentinos visit vendor
Listfully lap lemonade, lack lover

Desperate dudes desire daft darling dates
Wistful wishing wastes wondrous women's wants
Miserable men may miss mooning mates
Tipsy teasers tell terrible taunts

And another afternoon advances
Required rapport rescues real romances

Meant to say bye

I meant to say bye, I should have done that
When I mentioned love, knew that you would leave
All because of the wrong word in a chat
The closing of the door won't make me grieve

Love was keeping me around, we didn't share
Your idea of love is being owned
My idea of love is one to care
Want more than a heart that is only loaned

We are both better off this way I know
You can find someone to fit what you need
That kind of person always seems to show
Easily found all around like a weed

I will look for a love that could be true
Some think those seeking true love are too few

Cheshire in mind

Chin can always be found below a smile
Harboring dimples, kept securely there
Escalating beauty pass Queen of Nile.
Sitting above, framing your smile with care,
Holding that smile like hearts made to order
In Harmony above then below,
Rests your two lips, an exquisite border
Existing to let your breath through to flow

Immediately above, is a nose
Needed for smells identification

Made to crinkle cutely when need arose
Irresistibly above olefaction
Nestle your gorgeous eyes, all that in mind
Don't know why all I see is your smile kind

Lilacs

Heavenly scent engulfing all around
Essence of a pure sweetness fills the air
Replacing all year-round smells that are found
All about on Mackinac Island there

Insistence of beauty forced into your
Soul, mingling with all the other visions

That lie there, fills your life with their allure
Often found in dark purple, occasions

Live all over the island of bright white
Increasing in blue along the spectrum
Lilacs contain half a rainbow's delight
Allowing beauty to be a plectrum

Caressing our heart strings sweet as citrons
Sending out music sweeter than sirens